Good People Great Influence

A faith and confidence compilation of leadership and management attitude and influence.

Phil Larson gets called by the aliases of the think director, Dr. Dad, Dr. Phil, Guru, Teach, Boss, Hermano Filipe, and Mr. In-Plant, even though I never invented any of those. My most precious titles are husband, dad, and friend. After all, leadership and management start in our personal relationships. It is for life that we work.

40+ years of managing and still doing it.

Power Principles for Leaders:

Faced with an insurmountable company turnaround, we posted a set of leadership and management focus items in the main hallway of our department. The company was in chapter 11 bankruptcy. Failure to correct the issues was not an option if we intended to survive. As I examined these principles that helped us focus, it was obvious to me that they were based on ancient principles.

Here are ten tested core principles that mustered with faith will guide you through the worst of times and the best of times. I've been using them for over 3 decades in tough situations.

Your mission, should you decide to accept it, is to apply strong principles of faith and confidence to your own personal moments of decision to find amazing results that defy normal explanations.

Contents

Christian Power Living Tips!

Christians should be model employees and model employers. For that reason, I've included an entire section devoted to core Christian principles that should be lived in the workplace. Of course they are excellent for all, but essential for Christians.

Each starts with the admonition, Risk It! Faith requires risk. Risk is always involved in Faith. Faith is not fearsome nor ignorant. It is focused and responsible and Risky. The faith example you give is watched by those around you and influences them to greater vision and action.

Every section has a question for you to take inventory of your situation, a challenge for you to make application, and a prayer to help you activate your faith.

Risk It! Respect Authority

Take ancient authority into your workplace. Truths that transcend culture, industry, and size of business.

Psalm 19:1: The heavens declare the glory of God; and the firmament reveals openly his handywork.2: Day unto day cries out loudly with speech, and night unto night displays and reveals knowledge. 3: There is no speech nor language, where their voice is not heard.

A winner... respects those who are superior to him and tries to learn something from them.

A Loser resents those who are superior and rationalizes their achievements.

In 1980 a young student began to lose his ability to learn. The key instructor just did not seem to be passing anything on. What was the problem? The student had left home and job to study under this learned man. Travelling 500 miles, he had risked everything, and now he seemed to be learning nothing.

Self-examination revealed a loser's attitude toward the instructor. The student had begun to rationalize, see himself better than he was. Since he wasn't singled out and acknowledged, he began internally to tear at the credibility of the instructor. The door to knowledge closed.

The gateway of learning is opened when respect is in place.

Being a quick learner, the student adjusted. The next day he cornered the instructor and asked forgiveness. What? Ask forgiveness for a sin not committed? Yes. He asked for forgiveness from the instructor for holding anything between them. The gentle instructor forgave and forgot.

Psalm 86:5: You, Lord, are good and gracious and kind, and ready to forgive; and abundant in mercy to everyone that calls on you in their time of need.

Learning quickly returned. Now the wisdom of life flowed from instructor to student. The student went on to glean many critical lessons from this instructor which prospered him in life.

Proverbs 1:5: A wise man will hear, and will increase learning; and a man of understanding shall attain unto wise counsels:

Proverbs 1:7: The fear (respect and consideration of position and authority and person) of the LORD is the beginning (the opening of the doorway) of knowledge: but fools despise wisdom and instruction.

This principle applies not just to respecting the Lord but to respecting anyone.

Take Inventory: Do you have a lack of respect standing the way of knowledge in a relationship?

How can we be sensitive to remove the blocks to receiving knowledge and remove them quickly?

For whom do you have respect that is prospering your growth? Have you thanked that person recently?

Make Application: Write what you are going to specifically do in the next 30 days about this.

Pray Respect: *Shepherd of My Soul, guide me in a manner that respects and recognizes that You have positioned others over decisions in my life for good. Even when I am confused, You are in charge.*

The gateway of learning is opened when respect is in place.

Risk It! Explain Not Excuse

Romans 14:11: For it is written, as I live, says the Lord, every knee shall bow to me, and every tongue shall confess to God. 12: So then every one of us shall give account of himself to God. 13: Let us not therefore judge one another anymore: but judge this rather, that no man put a stumbling block or an occasion to fall in his brother's way

A winner explains; a loser explains away

Early in life I found it profitable to have solutions. Managers, directors, executives all seemed to be unconcerned with my problems and mistakes. What they wanted was solutions. Explain the problems and offer a solution. It really did not make a difference whether I caused the problem or not. A winner goes for the solution not the excuse.

God is the same way. He really is not so much interested in punishing us. **He is interested in our growth.**

This trait of offering honest explanations with solutions is called faithfulness. When we trust a person, we are honest. When we value their opinion in the long term, we are honest. Being that way adds up to being loyal and faithful and it is so returned.

In the computer industry of big systems, there are sometimes some real messes. Blaming it on the computer never flies. It always seems profitable to simply tell people, "We are researching the problem and will get back with you." And then do it.

Doctored Madness: A certain hospital had a horrible reputation. Systems crashed daily, sometimes 3 times a day. Nurses screamed. Doctors threatened to throw equipment out the window. One doctor would come into the computer room and bang on the equipment. When the system went down, all the technicians took off their badges and hid from the hospital staff.

As a new manager, Newbie was perplexed. How do you handle this mess? First, he instructed his technicians to get their badges back on and get into the hallways. Take the heat. Own up to the problems and help. Next, he called all the head nurses and gave them an estimate of when they could expect systems so they could go back to work. Then he called the chief technicians and wanted answers. **Real answers.** When it was all over, he would update the executives to the causes.

It was tough. The reputation of the department was horrid. Over time the nurses began to trust the reports. Even when it was bad news, it was trustworthy news. Systems started getting fixed and executives agreed to spend the right monies to fix the problems. Everyone turned out to be winners. Eventually the systems that were only up 50% of the time were up 98% of the time. Winners explain.

Good People Great Influence

I Corinthians 4:1: Let a man so account of us, as of the ministers of Christ, and stewards of the mysteries of God. 2: Moreover, it is required in stewards that a man be found faithful.

Watson's Venture: A story is told about Thomas Watson, then chief of IBM. Seems an executive spent a few million dollars on a project that was a total failure. He entered Watson's office thinking he would be terminated. Watson looked at him and assured him that he was not about to lose the millions he had invested in the man's training. He was not fired. He was trained to build solutions when troubles appeared.

What if he had offered excuses and blamed others? What if he had not been honest with his mistakes?

Adam had that type of opportunity. He blamed Eve. What if he had just told God he miffed it and needed forgiveness?

David, king of Israel, committed murder, adultery, and things we don't even know about. But when it came time to face it, he was **honest and simply explained**. God forgave and restored him each time. David wasn't perfect, he just would not try and explain away.

Hebrews. 13:17: Obey them that have the rule over you and submit yourselves: for they watch for your souls, as they that must give account, that they may do it with joy, and not with grief: for that is unprofitable for you.

This principle applies in all areas. **We all make mistakes.** We all have failures. (Failure is an event, not a person.) **We all are required to show faithfulness and loyalty by being honest and helping those around us deal with the situation.** They need the full scoop so they can work out any side issues, not punish or dig it in.

Take Inventory: Do you have a problem that needs fixing? Can you explain? Will you explain?

How can you get past the fear of failure through honest explanations?

Make Application: Write what you are going to specifically do in the next 30 days about this.

Pray To Be Honest in Explanation

Father, open my eyes. Let me see any hindrances to winning with Jesus. So many times, in life lessons go unlearned when I don't hear Your voice. Speak clearly, Lord. Let me hear and act speedily. Open my heart, Father, to give real, honest explanations so I can stay on the road to winning.

Risk It! Find A Way

Revelation 2:7: He that hath an ear, let him hear what the Spirit says to the churches; to him that overcomes will I give to eat of the tree of life, which is in the midst of the paradise of God.

A winner says, "Let's find a way."

A Loser says, "There is no way"

Philippians 4:13: I can do all things through Christ which strengthens me.

Problems are life. A great book written some years back is entitled, "Eating Problems for Breakfast." Another great book published years ago was "Lateral Thinking". Both books challenge us to remember that problem solving requires getting outside our normal boxes of thought and thinking different thoughts. When we are ready to do that, **we can see incredible solutions to plaguing problems.**

Kids In Bleachers: In the children's department of a large church, the problem of space for growth came up. The main area for elementary kids would only hold about 150 chairs, crammed uncomfortably with bad visibility. There had to be a way. After 15 years of looking at the problem, no one had a real viable solution. **It took getting outside the box.**

Walking through another room planned for remodeling a worker struck **an old idea with a new twist**. A choir loft seating about 75 adults was going to be torn out. Why not split the loft and reassemble it in the kids' area as bleachers? The new use of an old item would make room for 100 new kids. Not only that, but it took up little used space in the room and changed the room to a more exciting place for the kids and allowed over 250 kids to be in the room with all of them having good visibility. Add to that another idea of doubling the lumens in the lighting and the whole idea gelled. Unusable, dim space was turned into light, great space because some folks thought outside the box against 15 years of "no way".

Sunbonnet: The cost was only a few dollars as the labor was volunteered along with some great carpet to cover the bleachers. The cost of purchasing bleachers and installing a new lighting system would have been over $10,000. $10,000 may not seem like much but realize a group that for a group with no money, it was unrealistic.

1 Peter 1:7: That the trial (testing by presenting of problems) of your faith, being much more precious than of gold that perishes, though it be tried with fire, might be found unto praise and honor and glory at the appearing of Jesus Christ:

This principle applies in all areas of life. Tests, trials, opportunities, problems, glitches, frustrations, whatever you call them come up. **Persistent prayer and thought can bring new light (couldn't resist) and a different way**

to attack the problem. Faith pushes through to solutions. Fear stares at the problem and gives up.

Take Inventory: Do you have a long-term problem that needs fixing? How can you persist again and say, "There has to be a way!"?

What can you do today to get past the idea that you live with that old problem?

Make Application: Write what you are going to specifically do in the next 30 days about this.

Pray To Be A Problem Solver: *Father, quicken my mind and heart. Encourage faith in me to believe again for something on which I have given up hope. You are so real and alive and active in everything that is. Stretch my faith. Let me be like the one who said to Jesus, "Lord, I believe. Help my unbelief." Give me the courage to try a new approach and see Your hand displayed.*

Risk It! Go On Through.

To go through a problem is to conquer it and create new paths. Go through. Don't go around it.

Psalm 95:8: Harden not your heart, as in the provocation, and as in the day of temptation in the wilderness

A winner goes through a problem.

A loser tries to go around a problem.

Philippians 4:13: I can do all things through Christ which strengthens me.

Problems are life. Sound like the last chapter? You are right. It is not the same though. What makes a winner a conqueror and an overcomer, is the problems they face and conquer. You will have problems. *1Peter 4:12:" Beloved, think it not strange concerning the fiery trial, which is to try you, as though some strange thing happened unto you:"*

The question is will you go through or around?

Going around. The children of Israel spent 40 years going around their problems. When they were offered the land of opportunity, they chose to stay away and not deal with their problems. What was their problem? Discord, lack of submission to leadership, unbelief, and selfishness. Basically, they just had a lot of reliance on themselves and little on God.

Going through. After that 40-year phase, a new set of children rose up and went through their problems. They stuck together, defended each other, and took the blessings by going through their problems.

Going around. The United States is full of men and women going around their problems. Insecurity, lack of knowledge on how to be a dad/mom/husband/wife, lack of commitment, irresponsibility, and self-fulfillment keeps them from sticking with their families and spouses and friends. It's easier to get around.

Going through. My heroes are the ones who overcome their insecurities, lack of knowledge, lack of commitment, irresponsibility, and self-fulfillment, replace it with security in Jesus, knowledge from the Word, commitment to what counts, responsibility even when it hurts, other- fulfillment, and stick with the program. It is not easy. It is incredibly rewarding.

Hebrews 4:14: Seeing then that we have a great high priest, that is passed into the heavens, Jesus the Son of God, let us hold fast our profession.15: For we have not an high priest which cannot be touched with the feeling of our infirmities; but was in all points tempted like as we are, yet without sin.16: Let us therefore come boldly unto the throne of grace, that we may obtain mercy, and find grace to help in time of need.

Principle is principle is principle. Relationships, work issues, projects, and hobbies all present problems. When you allow others to help in the process, you prosper quicker. Sometimes they have the solution you need. Always, Jesus has the solution you need.

Take Inventory: Where do you have a problem that you have circumvented but not solved?

Are you ready to do what it takes to solve it?

Have you ever felt like getting mad at God because of a problem? Did you go around the problem or through it?

Overcoming. As I write this, I am praying for five relationships where someone has come to me in the last week and asked for prayer. They are GOING THROUGH! Anger, alcohol, and accusations make for hard lives. You can GO THROUGH. You can overcome. It takes both involved in the relationship, but it can be done. Who are you praying for?

Make Application

Write what you are going to specifically do in the next 30 days about this.

Pray for Push through Power: *Father of Strength and Conquest, Your word tells me those that follow You and Your way will do great exploits. We are not a common race. We are uncommonly filled with all the things necessary for life and for Godliness. Make me like You. Make me to be creative and persistent in all things to see solutions and fresh progress.*

Risk It! The Better Way Mentality

Every progressive effort starts with a step toward change and a holy dissatisfaction with the status quo.

Philipians3:13: Brethren, I count not myself to have apprehended: but this one thing I do, forgetting those things which are behind, and reaching forth unto those things which are before,

A winner ...says, "There is a better way."

A loser.... says, "That is the way it has always been done around here."

Philippians 4:13: I can do all things through Christ which strengthens me.

Life is full of opportunities to continue to do the same things. One man defined insanity this way: Doing the same thing over and over and expecting different results. Expectations, persistence of others, voices from the past, and other forces impugn our ability to think new, creative thoughts about what we do.

How do you get into the "better way" mentality? A favorite saying of mine is, **"If it ain't broke, break it."** What? Don't you mean, "If it ain't broke, don't fix it." No, I meant what I wrote. "If it ain't broke, break it." Many times, we build traditional barriers around an activity structured on preference and our limited understanding at the time. A man displayed curiosity about the way his wife cooked a roast beef. She would always cut the ends off. Thinking there must be a great culinary secret to this method he asked her why. "I don't know," she replied, "my mother taught me that way." Pressed for information on the private process he went to her mother. "I don't know," she replied, "my mother taught me that way." Perplexed he drove to the matron of the family's home and asked again. "Oh," she quickly responded, "my roasting pan was too short to hold the full roast."

Most processes need to be repaired regularly. Now, you don't want to tear up a good thing, so there are many other rules of change and improvement like: Always give a change time to go through the curve of lagging productivity until people learn the new way and become adept before implementing the next change. And any change will be resisted in strength in direct proportion to its' potential for improvement.

Life is full of processes and a "better way" mentality will protect you from foolish failure. A computer tech went out to resolve a problem one day in an executive secretary's office. Seemed that every time she printed a letter, she first had to print all the letters she had ever printed. It took a half a box of paper to print a letter! The cost and time of doing her job that way finally overcame her embarrassment and she asked for help. The fix was simple. She was simply doing what she had been shown. Open a file, go to the end, type the letter, and print it. The problem was she had only been given one file name and all the letters since she began her job were in one file that she printed each time according to explicit instructions.

Absurd? Real. Fortune 500 company. An executive secretary doing something that needed to be broken.

What about the way we converse with others? What about how we walk into a meeting? What about how we greet our friends? Are those processes that could use some "better way" mentality?

Jesus broke the mold for some in the way they treated their parents in a story related in Matthew 15. God gave a principle. Honor your fathers and mothers. The locals made a rule that kept them out of keeping the first rule conveniently. Tradition overruled wisdom and principle, and Jesus saw through the smoke. *Matt 15:6: Thus have ye made the commandment of God of none effect by your tradition.*

Therefore, since we are surrounded by such a great cloud of witnesses, let us throw off everything that hinders and the sin that so easily entangles, and let us run with perseverance the race marked out for us. Let us fix our eyes on Jesus, the author and perfecter of our faith, who for the joy set before him endured the cross, scorning its shame, and sat down at the right hand of the throne of God. Hebrews 12: 1-2 NIV.

Principle is principle is principle. Relationships, work issues, projects, and hobbies all present problems. When you allow others to help in the process, you prosper quicker. Sometimes they have the solution you need. **Always, Jesus has the solution you need.**

Take Inventory: Where do you have a process, a way of doing things that really could use some improvement by being broken?

Are you ready to give up personal preferences and do what it takes to "break it and make it better"?

Can you think of a scripture to apply that can help you into "better way" mentality?

Make Application: Write what you are going to specifically do in the next 30 days about this.

Pray To Be Changeable: *Father, quicken my mind and heart. Life is full of processes. You know the one that needs breaking and bettering at this moment. God, I can get so confused with all the items in life. What item can I work on today? What am I doing that really does more damage than good? Where can I get a lift seeing you touch a new area of my life and give me a creative fresh approach? Cleanse my thinking, Lord. Jesus, be my wisdom, be my source, be my life giver. Holy Spirit, release the fresh wind of Your brooding. Brood over my thoughts and bring order to their chaos that I might see clearly what You want to create.*

Risk It! Change

Every great innovation began with a resistance to the status quo. The greatest status quo that hinders is personal character.

Philippians 4:8: Finally, brethren, whatsoever things are true, whatsoever things are honest, whatsoever things are just, whatsoever things are pure, whatsoever things are lovely, whatsoever things are of good report; if there be any virtue, and if there be any praise, think on these things. 9: Those things, which ye have both learned, and received, and heard, and seen in me, do: and the God of peace shall be with you.

A winner ...shows he is sorry by acting differently.

A loser.... says, "I'm sorry", but continues to do it again.

Philippians 4:13: I can do all things through Christ who strengthens me.

You would like to get victory over weaknesses, wouldn't you? That is what Jesus is all about. In the book of Revelation there are many promises to the one who overcomes, stays until the end, "takes a lickin' and keeps on tickin", and keeps moving on. Our weaknesses, insecurities, nuances of personality haunt us in the path of the winner. Over and over, we will make mistakes, glitch in performance, slip climbing the ladder, fall on our face, and get egg on our face, boondoggle......sin.

Yes, **one key word used for sin in the Bible is simply to miss the mark.** Shoot at a goal and miss it. Decide we want to be loving and react with anger. Decide to keep our minds pure then fill it with trashy books, magazines, and the boob tube. Promise to a wife or son or daughter or friend or neighbor or coworker or employee or employer and then not follow through. Sin.

The question is, "What do we do then?" Do we take a winner's stance or a loser's escape? Do we face up, fess up, and clean the mess up? Or do we put on a face, say, "I'm sorry", and fade away only to do it again and again?

Winners change. **Winners find a way to do life differently the next time.**

Some years back a famous jewel thief was being interviewed over his life. He had spent many years in prison. His modus operandi was to only steal from the rich and famous. The interviewer asked him what his biggest theft was. His reply was, "Me." The explanation was simple. He had stolen his own life. What could have been a great creative mind used productively was used to steal and hurt. When you refuse to change and use the talents and strengths God gives you, you are stealing from yourself. Your time, energy, and talent go into actions that only produce hurt and pain for you and others. Why not change to a better way? Why not get a new thought process and quit doing what doesn't work, what only hurts?

Therefore, since we are surrounded by such a great cloud of witnesses, let us throw off everything that hinders and the sin that so easily entangles, and let us run with perseverance the race marked out for us. Let us fix our eyes on Jesus, the author and perfector of our faith, who for the joy set before him endured the cross, scorning its shame, and sat down at the right hand of the throne of God.   Hebrews 12: 1-2 NIV.

Take Inventory: What needs changing in your thought life?

What can you fill your mind with that will cause the old thoughts to go out and new ones come in?

Make a date with destiny. When are you going to start?

Make Application: Write what you are going to specifically do in the next 30 days about this.

Let's Pray: *Father, it is tough to give up my habits and hang-ups. I like them. They like me. They fit my life. Everyone who knows me, knows me as I am. And You want me to change. I need strength. Empower me with Your Holy Spirit*

Risk It! Stand Ground. Give Ground.

Pick your battles. There is a time to stand and a time to give ground. Use wisdom. Move purposefully.

Philippians 1:27: But whatever happens, make sure that your everyday life is worthy of the gospel of Christ. So that whether I do come and see you, or merely hear about you from a distance, I may know that you are standing fast in a united spirit, battling with a single mind for the faith of the gospel and not caring two straws for your enemies. (J.B. Phillips translation).

A winner..... Knows when to fight and when to compromise.

A loser ..... Fights over the wrong things and compromises at the wrong time.

Hebrews 12:14 Let it be your ambition to live at peace with all men and to achieve holiness "without which no man shall see the Lord" (J.B. Phillips translation)

Winners know when to fight to win and when to give. In the song, "The Gambler", the advice was given, "You got to know when to hold 'em, know when to fold 'em, know when to walk away, and know when to run." There is a fight worth fighting, and there are items in life not worth the effort.

29

Winston Churchill in the darkest hours of England's
battles with Germany had this sense. When others
wanted to lay down and give up, he stood ground and
challenged, "Never give up. Never give up. Never give
up." The war was won over courage and tenacity and
knowing the fight needed to be fought.

You must know when to fight. After living in their new
home for a year, the Newbies had a major
problem. Sewage came running over into the downstairs
bath, living room, and entry foyer. What a
mess! Massive cleanup, roto-rooter, and a few days of
showering at the neighbors did not fix it. The city
claimed the problem was theirs, the plumber claimed the
city needed to fix it. Two great neighbors and a day of
digging exposed a major city problem. Out they came,
and yes, they fixed it. They dug 14 feet deep, repaired the
sewer main, and replaced fences they had to tear
down. But they didn't take care of the carpet and
house. Forms, forms, and more forms, telephone calls,
working with city attorneys, and a lot of prayer resulted
in a surprise. One night the local city councilman called
to alert the Newbies that their reimbursement request
was scheduled to get the hatchet the next day at the city
council meeting. Newbie showed up at the council
meeting of this large metropolitan community. Deep in
the docket was a line item scratching the claim along
with over 30 other homeowners. What could he
do? Fight. Fight for his wife to get carpet. Fight for
restoration. Fight he did. First in prayer, then in

rhetoric. "Mayor, my friends and I dug a 7-foot-deep hole to show the city that the problem was theirs, I am willing to dig a 7-foot-deep rhetorical hole to help the council see it needs to pay these costs." The council halted him right there and offered to pay a reasonable settlement. No one else was awarded that day. The clerk could not believe it when she issued the check.

Know when to give and when to compromise. The budget battle was intense. Hundreds of thousands of dollars in expansion monies were battled over by several departments. Systems executives along with Newbie decided to withdraw and let the money go to retail remodels. Eight months later accounting in an executive meeting moved $50,000.00 to systems and challenged them, "See what you can do with that." After 30 days of scrambling and results, they gave them another $400,000.00 to spend moved from retail remodels.

Take Inventory: Where do you need to fight? Does someone need defending?

Where do you need to lay down your arms? Is it better to give now and win a friend?

Make Application: Write what you are going to specifically do in the next 30 days about this.

Let's Pray: *Okay, God of Glory, Lord of Hosts (Armies Camped for War), I need Your wisdom. There is a time to stand and a time to sit. There is a time to run forward and a time to hold present ground. Show me the most effective use of my time right now. Give me courage to engage the enemy for good in all areas of my life.*

Risk It!

Winners take risks. They are unafraid of loss. The balance of gains over losses motivates.

Psalm 20:6: Now I know that the LORD saves (brings out of trouble, restores, and strengthens) His anointed; He will hear him (and respond to his rallying call for help) from His holy heaven with the saving strength of His right hand (the hand of power and ability, the hand at which Jesus represents His). 7: Some trust in chariots, and some in horses (some trust in their riches and alliances and abilities and mental acuity): but we will remember the name of the LORD our God. 8: They (our enemies and all those who trust in their own strength) are brought down and fallen: but we are risen and stand upright.

Winners are not afraid of losing or making mistakes.

They are willing to take risks necessary to succeed in life.

Life means risk. Life means taking chances that cause loss. Loss of friends, loss of co-workers, loss of status, loss of power, loss of control, loss of understanding of those important to you, loss of money. All these are losses a winner decides at times must be risked. "No pain, no gain. Know gain, know pain." some would say. Life means risk. Risk means loss. Risk also means winning.

Edison risked until he found the right element for light bulbs. Once on a comment that it took several thousand tries before he got results, he explained, "Results? Why I have gotten a lot of results. I know thousands of things that won't work."

Ray Kroc became an outstanding business leader. Yet, for years he failed at every business attempt. It was so bad his wife was ready to leave him on his last venture. Seems he sold everything to buy a few hamburger joints owned by some brothers named McDonald. You guessed it. That was the start of the McDonald's chain of restaurants that made the Krocs multi-millionaires. Winners keep trying. (By the way, his wife stuck it out.)

Those secure in Jesus are unafraid of risk because they know He will back them up. They know they can make a mistake and be put back on track.

Psalm 37:23: The steps of a good man are ordered by the LORD: and he delights in his way. 24: Though he fall, he shall not be utterly cast down: for the LORD upholds him with his hand. 25: I have been young, and now am old; yet have I not seen the righteous forsaken, nor his seed begging bread. 26: He is ever merciful and lends; and his seed is blessed.

Take Inventory: Pensive?

Trying to decide?

What is it?

Write it down. Write down the good and bad things about it. Pray about it. Listen to God. Commit it to Him. Decide. Don't let fear hold you down.

Make Application: Write what you are going to specifically do in the next 30 days about this.

Pray To Be Bold: *Father, encourage me. Strengthen me to take that step of faith in Your leading. I am weak, Father. I fail. I am made of grass and wither in the noon sun, but You cause a shadow to cover me. Let the cool breath of Your Spirit blow over me and freshen my day. Though I fall, I will get up and go again. You will cause me to succeed.*

Risk It! Be an Able Also.

The intensity of being a contributor versus a consumer brings us to moments of challenged ability. Be one that is **able in the moment needed** and others will entrust greatness into your hands.

2 Timothy 2:2: And the things that thou hast heard of me among many witnesses, the same commit thou to faithful men, who shall be able to teach others also.

Winners Make Commitments.

Losers Make Promises.

In these few short words to Timothy, Paul revealed a tremendous portion of the key to his winning life. Look at the word choices. Among Many Witnesses. The Same. Commit. Faithful Men. Able Also.

Among many witnesses. **Paul was not afraid for his life to be tested against witnesses**. His words were true, and he stayed with them. What witnesses heard years before still was true of his life. Timothy was charged to make sure solid teaching, life, and words passed on to other men of commitment.

The same. **Paul was open in his life**. He committed himself to being like Jesus. The same yesterday, today, and forever.

Commit. Paul was committal. **He made commitments and expected others to do the same.**

Faithful men. These are hard to find. **Paul never gave up.** Betrayed continually, he never gave up looking for faithful men.

Able also. We can be "able also". **An "able also" does the same in making commitment, sticking with it, being faithful, following through, endures all things, bears all things, believes all things, hopes all things.**

Promises are cheap. "I'll be there." MEANS "If it fits the pressures of the moment's right before." OR "Whatever it takes to get you to quit asking." "Til death do us part." MEANS "Until I redefine what I meant." OR "Until I don't want to handle the pressures anymore face to face."

Commitment is expensive. "I'll be there." MEANS "Whatever the cost, I'll rearrange life to get me there." "Til death do us part." MEANS "I will stick it out though I may not feel like it. "I will take control of my feelings and bring them to submission in Christ."

*Psalm 15:1: LORD, who shall abide in thy tabernacle? Who shall dwell in thy holy hill? 2: He that **walks uprightly**, and works righteousness, and **speaks the truth in his heart.** 3: He that backbites not with his tongue, nor does evil to his neighbor, nor takes up a reproach against his neighbor. 4: In whose eyes a vile person is contemned; but he honors them that fear the LORD. **He that swears to his own hurt, and*** *changes not. 5: He that puts not out his money to usury, nor taketh reward against the innocent. He that doeth these things shall never be moved.*

Take Inventory: What does it mean to be an "ABLE ALSO"?

What changes do I have to make?

Are there repairs that need to be done to broken commitments?

When am I willing to start?

Make Application: Write what you are going to specifically do in the next 30 days about this.

Pray To Be an Able Also

Father, make me an "ABLE ALSO". Change the way I promise to commitment. Instill in me faithfulness. When I am faithless, You are faith-full. Make me like Jesus, the same yesterday, today, and forever. Psalm 51:10: Create in me a clean heart, O God; and renew a right spirit within me. 11: Cast me not away from thy presence; and take not thy holy spirit from me. 12: Restore unto me the joy of thy salvation; and uphold me with thy free spirit. 13: Then will I teach transgressors thy ways; and sinners shall be converted unto thee.

Prologue

There you are. Ten key principles of faith and confident rei

You can read more about Good People in the book series Just Regular People on Amazon.

Join me on LinkedIn (phillarsonokc)

Find me on Facebook. (solumcommunity.net)

Read online solumcommunity.net

We Own the Future! Tenemos El Futuro.

www.ingramcontent.com/pod-product-compliance
Lightning Source LLC
Chambersburg PA
CBHW071017290526
45795CB00005B/1841